# PERSONAL INFORMATION

| | |
|---|---|
| Name | |
| Email | |
| Address | |
| Phone Number | |

# EMERGENCY CONTACT

| | |
|---|---|
| Name | |
| Phone Number | |

# LOG BOOK DETAILS

| | |
|---|---|
| Log Start Date | |
| Log Book Number | |

Notes: _____

_____

_____

_____

_____

_____

_____

# Table of Contents

# Visitation Planner

# January

| DATE | PICK UP | | DROP OFF | | NOTES |
|---|---|---|---|---|---|
| | TIME | LOCATION | TIME | LOCATION | |
| | | | | | |
| | | | | | |
| | | | | | |
| | | | | | |
| | | | | | |
| | | | | | |
| | | | | | |
| | | | | | |
| | | | | | |
| | | | | | |
| | | | | | |
| | | | | | |
| | | | | | |
| | | | | | |
| | | | | | |
| | | | | | |
| | | | | | |
| | | | | | |
| | | | | | |
| | | | | | |
| | | | | | |
| | | | | | |
| | | | | | |
| | | | | | |
| | | | | | |
| | | | | | |
| | | | | | |
| | | | | | |
| | | | | | |
| | | | | | |
| | | | | | |
| | | | | | |
| | | | | | |

# Visitation Planner

## February

| DATE | PICK UP | | DROP OFF | | NOTES |
|------|---------|--------|----------|----------|-------|
| | TIME | LOCATION | TIME | LOCATION | |
| | | | | | |
| | | | | | |
| | | | | | |
| | | | | | |
| | | | | | |
| | | | | | |
| | | | | | |
| | | | | | |
| | | | | | |
| | | | | | |
| | | | | | |
| | | | | | |
| | | | | | |
| | | | | | |
| | | | | | |
| | | | | | |
| | | | | | |
| | | | | | |
| | | | | | |
| | | | | | |
| | | | | | |
| | | | | | |
| | | | | | |
| | | | | | |
| | | | | | |
| | | | | | |
| | | | | | |
| | | | | | |
| | | | | | |
| | | | | | |

# Visitation Planner

| DATE | PICK UP | | DROP OFF | | NOTES |
|------|---------|----------|----------|----------|-------|
|      | TIME | LOCATION | TIME | LOCATION |       |
|      |      |          |      |          |       |
|      |      |          |      |          |       |
|      |      |          |      |          |       |
|      |      |          |      |          |       |
|      |      |          |      |          |       |
|      |      |          |      |          |       |
|      |      |          |      |          |       |
|      |      |          |      |          |       |
|      |      |          |      |          |       |
|      |      |          |      |          |       |
|      |      |          |      |          |       |
|      |      |          |      |          |       |
|      |      |          |      |          |       |
|      |      |          |      |          |       |
|      |      |          |      |          |       |
|      |      |          |      |          |       |
|      |      |          |      |          |       |
|      |      |          |      |          |       |
|      |      |          |      |          |       |
|      |      |          |      |          |       |
|      |      |          |      |          |       |
|      |      |          |      |          |       |
|      |      |          |      |          |       |
|      |      |          |      |          |       |
|      |      |          |      |          |       |
|      |      |          |      |          |       |
|      |      |          |      |          |       |
|      |      |          |      |          |       |
|      |      |          |      |          |       |
|      |      |          |      |          |       |
|      |      |          |      |          |       |
|      |      |          |      |          |       |
|      |      |          |      |          |       |

# Visitation Planner

## April

| DATE | PICK UP | | DROP OFF | | NOTES |
|------|---------|---------|---------|---------|-------|
| | TIME | LOCATION | TIME | LOCATION | |
| | | | | | |
| | | | | | |
| | | | | | |
| | | | | | |
| | | | | | |
| | | | | | |
| | | | | | |
| | | | | | |
| | | | | | |
| | | | | | |
| | | | | | |
| | | | | | |
| | | | | | |
| | | | | | |
| | | | | | |
| | | | | | |
| | | | | | |
| | | | | | |
| | | | | | |
| | | | | | |
| | | | | | |
| | | | | | |
| | | | | | |
| | | | | | |
| | | | | | |
| | | | | | |
| | | | | | |
| | | | | | |
| | | | | | |
| | | | | | |
| | | | | | |
| | | | | | |

# Visitation Planner

| DATE | PICK UP | | DROP OFF | | NOTES |
|---|---|---|---|---|---|
| | TIME | LOCATION | TIME | LOCATION | |
| | | | | | |
| | | | | | |
| | | | | | |
| | | | | | |
| | | | | | |
| | | | | | |
| | | | | | |
| | | | | | |
| | | | | | |
| | | | | | |
| | | | | | |
| | | | | | |
| | | | | | |
| | | | | | |
| | | | | | |
| | | | | | |
| | | | | | |
| | | | | | |
| | | | | | |
| | | | | | |
| | | | | | |
| | | | | | |
| | | | | | |
| | | | | | |
| | | | | | |
| | | | | | |
| | | | | | |
| | | | | | |
| | | | | | |
| | | | | | |
| | | | | | |
| | | | | | |
| | | | | | |

# Visitation Planner

| DATE | PICK UP | | DROP OFF | | NOTES |
|------|---------|---|----------|---|-------|
|      | TIME | LOCATION | TIME | LOCATION |  |
|      |      |      |      |      |      |
|      |      |      |      |      |      |
|      |      |      |      |      |      |
|      |      |      |      |      |      |
|      |      |      |      |      |      |
|      |      |      |      |      |      |
|      |      |      |      |      |      |
|      |      |      |      |      |      |
|      |      |      |      |      |      |
|      |      |      |      |      |      |
|      |      |      |      |      |      |
|      |      |      |      |      |      |
|      |      |      |      |      |      |
|      |      |      |      |      |      |
|      |      |      |      |      |      |
|      |      |      |      |      |      |
|      |      |      |      |      |      |
|      |      |      |      |      |      |
|      |      |      |      |      |      |
|      |      |      |      |      |      |
|      |      |      |      |      |      |
|      |      |      |      |      |      |
|      |      |      |      |      |      |
|      |      |      |      |      |      |
|      |      |      |      |      |      |
|      |      |      |      |      |      |
|      |      |      |      |      |      |
|      |      |      |      |      |      |
|      |      |      |      |      |      |
|      |      |      |      |      |      |

# Visitation Planner

| DATE | PICK UP | | DROP OFF | | NOTES |
|------|---------|----------|----------|----------|-------|
| | TIME | LOCATION | TIME | LOCATION | |
| | | | | | |
| | | | | | |
| | | | | | |
| | | | | | |
| | | | | | |
| | | | | | |
| | | | | | |
| | | | | | |
| | | | | | |
| | | | | | |
| | | | | | |
| | | | | | |
| | | | | | |
| | | | | | |
| | | | | | |
| | | | | | |
| | | | | | |
| | | | | | |
| | | | | | |
| | | | | | |
| | | | | | |
| | | | | | |
| | | | | | |
| | | | | | |
| | | | | | |
| | | | | | |
| | | | | | |
| | | | | | |
| | | | | | |
| | | | | | |
| | | | | | |
| | | | | | |
| | | | | | |
| | | | | | |

# Visitation Planner

## August

| DATE | PICK UP | | DROP OFF | | NOTES |
|------|---------|----------|----------|----------|-------|
| | TIME | LOCATION | TIME | LOCATION | |
| | | | | | |
| | | | | | |
| | | | | | |
| | | | | | |
| | | | | | |
| | | | | | |
| | | | | | |
| | | | | | |
| | | | | | |
| | | | | | |
| | | | | | |
| | | | | | |
| | | | | | |
| | | | | | |
| | | | | | |
| | | | | | |
| | | | | | |
| | | | | | |
| | | | | | |
| | | | | | |
| | | | | | |
| | | | | | |
| | | | | | |
| | | | | | |
| | | | | | |
| | | | | | |
| | | | | | |
| | | | | | |
| | | | | | |
| | | | | | |
| | | | | | |

# Visitation Planner

# September

| DATE | PICK UP | | DROP OFF | | NOTES |
|------|---------|----------|----------|----------|-------|
| | TIME | LOCATION | TIME | LOCATION | |
| | | | | | |
| | | | | | |
| | | | | | |
| | | | | | |
| | | | | | |
| | | | | | |
| | | | | | |
| | | | | | |
| | | | | | |
| | | | | | |
| | | | | | |
| | | | | | |
| | | | | | |
| | | | | | |
| | | | | | |
| | | | | | |
| | | | | | |
| | | | | | |
| | | | | | |
| | | | | | |
| | | | | | |
| | | | | | |
| | | | | | |
| | | | | | |
| | | | | | |
| | | | | | |
| | | | | | |
| | | | | | |
| | | | | | |
| | | | | | |
| | | | | | |
| | | | | | |

# Visitation Planner

## October

| DATE | PICK UP | | DROP OFF | | NOTES |
|------|---------|----------|----------|----------|-------|
| | TIME | LOCATION | TIME | LOCATION | |
| | | | | | |
| | | | | | |
| | | | | | |
| | | | | | |
| | | | | | |
| | | | | | |
| | | | | | |
| | | | | | |
| | | | | | |
| | | | | | |
| | | | | | |
| | | | | | |
| | | | | | |
| | | | | | |
| | | | | | |
| | | | | | |
| | | | | | |
| | | | | | |
| | | | | | |
| | | | | | |
| | | | | | |
| | | | | | |
| | | | | | |
| | | | | | |
| | | | | | |
| | | | | | |
| | | | | | |
| | | | | | |
| | | | | | |
| | | | | | |
| | | | | | |

# Visitation Planner

## November

| DATE | PICK UP | | DROP OFF | | NOTES |
|------|---------|----------|----------|----------|-------|
| | TIME | LOCATION | TIME | LOCATION | |
| | | | | | |
| | | | | | |
| | | | | | |
| | | | | | |
| | | | | | |
| | | | | | |
| | | | | | |
| | | | | | |
| | | | | | |
| | | | | | |
| | | | | | |
| | | | | | |
| | | | | | |
| | | | | | |
| | | | | | |
| | | | | | |
| | | | | | |
| | | | | | |
| | | | | | |
| | | | | | |
| | | | | | |
| | | | | | |
| | | | | | |
| | | | | | |
| | | | | | |
| | | | | | |
| | | | | | |
| | | | | | |
| | | | | | |
| | | | | | |
| | | | | | |
| | | | | | |

# Visitation Planner

## December

| DATE | PICK UP | | DROP OFF | | NOTES |
|------|---------|----------|----------|----------|-------|
| | TIME | LOCATION | TIME | LOCATION | |
| | | | | | |
| | | | | | |
| | | | | | |
| | | | | | |
| | | | | | |
| | | | | | |
| | | | | | |
| | | | | | |
| | | | | | |
| | | | | | |
| | | | | | |
| | | | | | |
| | | | | | |
| | | | | | |
| | | | | | |
| | | | | | |
| | | | | | |
| | | | | | |
| | | | | | |
| | | | | | |
| | | | | | |
| | | | | | |
| | | | | | |
| | | | | | |
| | | | | | |
| | | | | | |
| | | | | | |
| | | | | | |
| | | | | | |
| | | | | | |

# Visitation Details

| Date: | | M T W T F S S |
|---|---|---|
| Child(ren)'s name: | | |
| Child(ren)'s age: | | |
| Agreed Pick Up Time: | Agreed Drop Off Time: | |
| Actual Pick Up Time: | Actual Drop Off Time: | |
| Location: | Location: | |
| Custodian Name: | Relationship to child: | |
| Contact Info: | | Signature: |
| Witness Name: | | Signature: |
| Notes: | | |

| Date: | | M T W T F S S |
|---|---|---|
| Child(ren)'s name: | | |
| Child(ren)'s age: | | |
| Agreed Pick Up Time: | Agreed Drop Off Time: | |
| Actual Pick Up Time: | Actual Drop Off Time: | |
| Location: | Location: | |
| Custodian Name: | Relationship to child: | |
| Contact Info: | | Signature: |
| Witness Name: | | Signature: |
| Notes: | | |

| Date: | | M T W T F S S |
|---|---|---|
| Child(ren)'s name: | | |
| Child(ren)'s age: | | |
| Agreed Pick Up Time: | Agreed Drop Off Time: | |
| Actual Pick Up Time: | Actual Drop Off Time: | |
| Location: | Location: | |
| Custodian Name: | Relationship to child: | |
| Contact Info: | | Signature: |
| Witness Name: | | Signature: |
| Notes: | | |

# Visitation Details

| Date: | | | | M | T | W | T | F | S | S |
|---|---|---|---|---|---|---|---|---|---|---|
| Child(ren)'s name: | | | | | | | | | | |
| Child(ren)'s age: | | | | | | | | | | |
| Agreed Pick Up Time: | | | Agreed Drop Off Time: | | | | | | | |
| Actual Pick Up Time: | | | Actual Drop Off Time: | | | | | | | |
| Location: | | | Location: | | | | | | | |
| Custodian Name: | | | Relationship to child: | | | | | | | |
| Contact Info: | | | | Signature: | | | | | | |
| Witness Name: | | | | Signature: | | | | | | |
| Notes: | | | | | | | | | | |

| Date: | | | | M | T | W | T | F | S | S |
|---|---|---|---|---|---|---|---|---|---|---|
| Child(ren)'s name: | | | | | | | | | | |
| Child(ren)'s age: | | | | | | | | | | |
| Agreed Pick Up Time: | | | Agreed Drop Off Time: | | | | | | | |
| Actual Pick Up Time: | | | Actual Drop Off Time: | | | | | | | |
| Location: | | | Location: | | | | | | | |
| Custodian Name: | | | Relationship to child: | | | | | | | |
| Contact Info: | | | | Signature: | | | | | | |
| Witness Name: | | | | Signature: | | | | | | |
| Notes: | | | | | | | | | | |

| Date: | | | | M | T | W | T | F | S | S |
|---|---|---|---|---|---|---|---|---|---|---|
| Child(ren)'s name: | | | | | | | | | | |
| Child(ren)'s age: | | | | | | | | | | |
| Agreed Pick Up Time: | | | Agreed Drop Off Time: | | | | | | | |
| Actual Pick Up Time: | | | Actual Drop Off Time: | | | | | | | |
| Location: | | | Location: | | | | | | | |
| Custodian Name: | | | Relationship to child: | | | | | | | |
| Contact Info: | | | | Signature: | | | | | | |
| Witness Name: | | | | Signature: | | | | | | |
| Notes: | | | | | | | | | | |

# Visitation Details

| Date: | | M T W T F S S |
|---|---|---|
| Child(ren)'s name: | | |
| Child(ren)'s age: | | |
| Agreed Pick Up Time: | Agreed Drop Off Time: | |
| Actual Pick Up Time: | Actual Drop Off Time: | |
| Location: | Location: | |
| Custodian Name: | Relationship to child: | |
| Contact Info: | | Signature: |
| Witness Name: | | Signature: |
| Notes: | | |

| Date: | | M T W T F S S |
|---|---|---|
| Child(ren)'s name: | | |
| Child(ren)'s age: | | |
| Agreed Pick Up Time: | Agreed Drop Off Time: | |
| Actual Pick Up Time: | Actual Drop Off Time: | |
| Location: | Location: | |
| Custodian Name: | Relationship to child: | |
| Contact Info: | | Signature: |
| Witness Name: | | Signature: |
| Notes: | | |

| Date: | | M T W T F S S |
|---|---|---|
| Child(ren)'s name: | | |
| Child(ren)'s age: | | |
| Agreed Pick Up Time: | Agreed Drop Off Time: | |
| Actual Pick Up Time: | Actual Drop Off Time: | |
| Location: | Location: | |
| Custodian Name: | Relationship to child: | |
| Contact Info: | | Signature: |
| Witness Name: | | Signature: |
| Notes: | | |

# Visitation Details

| Date: | | M   T   W   T   F   S   S |
|---|---|---|
| Child(ren)'s name: | | |
| Child(ren)'s age: | | |
| Agreed Pick Up Time: | Agreed Drop Off Time: | |
| Actual Pick Up Time: | Actual Drop Off Time: | |
| Location: | Location: | |
| Custodian Name: | Relationship to child: | |
| Contact Info: | Signature: | |
| Witness Name: | Signature: | |
| Notes: | | |

| Date: | | M   T   W   T   F   S   S |
|---|---|---|
| Child(ren)'s name: | | |
| Child(ren)'s age: | | |
| Agreed Pick Up Time: | Agreed Drop Off Time: | |
| Actual Pick Up Time: | Actual Drop Off Time: | |
| Location: | Location: | |
| Custodian Name: | Relationship to child: | |
| Contact Info: | Signature: | |
| Witness Name: | Signature: | |
| Notes: | | |

| Date: | | M   T   W   T   F   S   S |
|---|---|---|
| Child(ren)'s name: | | |
| Child(ren)'s age: | | |
| Agreed Pick Up Time: | Agreed Drop Off Time: | |
| Actual Pick Up Time: | Actual Drop Off Time: | |
| Location: | Location: | |
| Custodian Name: | Relationship to child: | |
| Contact Info: | Signature: | |
| Witness Name: | Signature: | |
| Notes: | | |

# Visitation Details

| Date: | | M | T | W | T | F | S | S |
|---|---|---|---|---|---|---|---|---|
| Child(ren)'s name: | | | | | | | | |
| Child(ren)'s age: | | | | | | | | |

| Agreed Pick Up Time: | Agreed Drop Off Time: |
|---|---|
| Actual Pick Up Time: | Actual Drop Off Time: |
| Location: | Location: |
| Custodian Name: | Relationship to child: |
| Contact Info: | Signature: |
| Witness Name: | Signature: |
| Notes: | |

| Date: | | M | T | W | T | F | S | S |
|---|---|---|---|---|---|---|---|---|
| Child(ren)'s name: | | | | | | | | |
| Child(ren)'s age: | | | | | | | | |

| Agreed Pick Up Time: | Agreed Drop Off Time: |
|---|---|
| Actual Pick Up Time: | Actual Drop Off Time: |
| Location: | Location: |
| Custodian Name: | Relationship to child: |
| Contact Info: | Signature: |
| Witness Name: | Signature: |
| Notes: | |

| Date: | | M | T | W | T | F | S | S |
|---|---|---|---|---|---|---|---|---|
| Child(ren)'s name: | | | | | | | | |
| Child(ren)'s age: | | | | | | | | |

| Agreed Pick Up Time: | Agreed Drop Off Time: |
|---|---|
| Actual Pick Up Time: | Actual Drop Off Time: |
| Location: | Location: |
| Custodian Name: | Relationship to child: |
| Contact Info: | Signature: |
| Witness Name: | Signature: |
| Notes: | |

# Visitation Details

| Date: | | M | T | W | T | F | S | S |
|---|---|---|---|---|---|---|---|---|
| Child(ren)'s name: | | | | | | | | |
| Child(ren)'s age: | | | | | | | | |
| Agreed Pick Up Time: | Agreed Drop Off Time: | | | | | | | |
| Actual Pick Up Time: | Actual Drop Off Time: | | | | | | | |
| Location: | Location: | | | | | | | |
| Custodian Name: | Relationship to child: | | | | | | | |
| Contact Info: | | Signature: | | | | | | |
| Witness Name: | | Signature: | | | | | | |
| Notes: | | | | | | | | |

| Date: | | M | T | W | T | F | S | S |
|---|---|---|---|---|---|---|---|---|
| Child(ren)'s name: | | | | | | | | |
| Child(ren)'s age: | | | | | | | | |
| Agreed Pick Up Time: | Agreed Drop Off Time: | | | | | | | |
| Actual Pick Up Time: | Actual Drop Off Time: | | | | | | | |
| Location: | Location: | | | | | | | |
| Custodian Name: | Relationship to child: | | | | | | | |
| Contact Info: | | Signature: | | | | | | |
| Witness Name: | | Signature: | | | | | | |
| Notes: | | | | | | | | |

| Date: | | M | T | W | T | F | S | S |
|---|---|---|---|---|---|---|---|---|
| Child(ren)'s name: | | | | | | | | |
| Child(ren)'s age: | | | | | | | | |
| Agreed Pick Up Time: | Agreed Drop Off Time: | | | | | | | |
| Actual Pick Up Time: | Actual Drop Off Time: | | | | | | | |
| Location: | Location: | | | | | | | |
| Custodian Name: | Relationship to child: | | | | | | | |
| Contact Info: | | Signature: | | | | | | |
| Witness Name: | | Signature: | | | | | | |
| Notes: | | | | | | | | |

# Visitation Details

| Date: | | M T W T F S S |
|---|---|---|
| Child(ren)'s name: | | |
| Child(ren)'s age: | | |
| Agreed Pick Up Time: | Agreed Drop Off Time: | |
| Actual Pick Up Time: | Actual Drop Off Time: | |
| Location: | Location: | |
| Custodian Name: | Relationship to child: | |
| Contact Info: | | Signature: |
| Witness Name: | | Signature: |
| Notes: | | |

| Date: | | M T W T F S S |
|---|---|---|
| Child(ren)'s name: | | |
| Child(ren)'s age: | | |
| Agreed Pick Up Time: | Agreed Drop Off Time: | |
| Actual Pick Up Time: | Actual Drop Off Time: | |
| Location: | Location: | |
| Custodian Name: | Relationship to child: | |
| Contact Info: | | Signature: |
| Witness Name: | | Signature: |
| Notes: | | |

| Date: | | M T W T F S S |
|---|---|---|
| Child(ren)'s name: | | |
| Child(ren)'s age: | | |
| Agreed Pick Up Time: | Agreed Drop Off Time: | |
| Actual Pick Up Time: | Actual Drop Off Time: | |
| Location: | Location: | |
| Custodian Name: | Relationship to child: | |
| Contact Info: | | Signature: |
| Witness Name: | | Signature: |
| Notes: | | |

# Visitation Details

| Date: | | M  T  W  T  F  S  S |
|---|---|---|
| Child(ren)'s name: | | |
| Child(ren)'s age: | | |
| Agreed Pick Up Time: | Agreed Drop Off Time: | |
| Actual Pick Up Time: | Actual Drop Off Time: | |
| Location: | Location: | |
| Custodian Name: | Relationship to child: | |
| Contact Info: | | Signature: |
| Witness Name: | | Signature: |
| Notes: | | |

| Date: | | M  T  W  T  F  S  S |
|---|---|---|
| Child(ren)'s name: | | |
| Child(ren)'s age: | | |
| Agreed Pick Up Time: | Agreed Drop Off Time: | |
| Actual Pick Up Time: | Actual Drop Off Time: | |
| Location: | Location: | |
| Custodian Name: | Relationship to child: | |
| Contact Info: | | Signature: |
| Witness Name: | | Signature: |
| Notes: | | |

| Date: | | M  T  W  T  F  S  S |
|---|---|---|
| Child(ren)'s name: | | |
| Child(ren)'s age: | | |
| Agreed Pick Up Time: | Agreed Drop Off Time: | |
| Actual Pick Up Time: | Actual Drop Off Time: | |
| Location: | Location: | |
| Custodian Name: | Relationship to child: | |
| Contact Info: | | Signature: |
| Witness Name: | | Signature: |
| Notes: | | |

# Visitation Details

| Date: | M T W T F S S |
|---|---|
| Child(ren)'s name: | |
| Child(ren)'s age: | |

| Agreed Pick Up Time: | Agreed Drop Off Time: | |
|---|---|---|
| Actual Pick Up Time: | Actual Drop Off Time: | |
| Location: | Location: | |
| Custodian Name: | Relationship to child: | |
| Contact Info: | | Signature: |
| Witness Name: | | Signature: |
| Notes: | | |

| Date: | M T W T F S S |
|---|---|
| Child(ren)'s name: | |
| Child(ren)'s age: | |

| Agreed Pick Up Time: | Agreed Drop Off Time: | |
|---|---|---|
| Actual Pick Up Time: | Actual Drop Off Time: | |
| Location: | Location: | |
| Custodian Name: | Relationship to child: | |
| Contact Info: | | Signature: |
| Witness Name: | | Signature: |
| Notes: | | |

| Date: | M T W T F S S |
|---|---|
| Child(ren)'s name: | |
| Child(ren)'s age: | |

| Agreed Pick Up Time: | Agreed Drop Off Time: | |
|---|---|---|
| Actual Pick Up Time: | Actual Drop Off Time: | |
| Location: | Location: | |
| Custodian Name: | Relationship to child: | |
| Contact Info: | | Signature: |
| Witness Name: | | Signature: |
| Notes: | | |

# Visitation Details

| Date: | | M  T  W  T  F  S  S |
|---|---|---|
| Child(ren)'s name: | | |
| Child(ren)'s age: | | |
| Agreed Pick Up Time: | Agreed Drop Off Time: | |
| Actual Pick Up Time: | Actual Drop Off Time: | |
| Location: | Location: | |
| Custodian Name: | Relationship to child: | |
| Contact Info: | | Signature: |
| Witness Name: | | Signature: |
| Notes: | | |

| Date: | | M  T  W  T  F  S  S |
|---|---|---|
| Child(ren)'s name: | | |
| Child(ren)'s age: | | |
| Agreed Pick Up Time: | Agreed Drop Off Time: | |
| Actual Pick Up Time: | Actual Drop Off Time: | |
| Location: | Location: | |
| Custodian Name: | Relationship to child: | |
| Contact Info: | | Signature: |
| Witness Name: | | Signature: |
| Notes: | | |

| Date: | | M  T  W  T  F  S  S |
|---|---|---|
| Child(ren)'s name: | | |
| Child(ren)'s age: | | |
| Agreed Pick Up Time: | Agreed Drop Off Time: | |
| Actual Pick Up Time: | Actual Drop Off Time: | |
| Location: | Location: | |
| Custodian Name: | Relationship to child: | |
| Contact Info: | | Signature: |
| Witness Name: | | Signature: |
| Notes: | | |

# Visitation Details

| Date: | | M   T   W   T   F   S   S |
|---|---|---|
| Child(ren)'s name: | | |
| Child(ren)'s age: | | |
| Agreed Pick Up Time: | Agreed Drop Off Time: | |
| Actual Pick Up Time: | Actual Drop Off Time: | |
| Location: | Location: | |
| Custodian Name: | Relationship to child: | |
| Contact Info: | | Signature: |
| Witness Name: | | Signature: |
| Notes: | | |

| Date: | | M   T   W   T   F   S   S |
|---|---|---|
| Child(ren)'s name: | | |
| Child(ren)'s age: | | |
| Agreed Pick Up Time: | Agreed Drop Off Time: | |
| Actual Pick Up Time: | Actual Drop Off Time: | |
| Location: | Location: | |
| Custodian Name: | Relationship to child: | |
| Contact Info: | | Signature: |
| Witness Name: | | Signature: |
| Notes: | | |

| Date: | | M   T   W   T   F   S   S |
|---|---|---|
| Child(ren)'s name: | | |
| Child(ren)'s age: | | |
| Agreed Pick Up Time: | Agreed Drop Off Time: | |
| Actual Pick Up Time: | Actual Drop Off Time: | |
| Location: | Location: | |
| Custodian Name: | Relationship to child: | |
| Contact Info: | | Signature: |
| Witness Name: | | Signature: |
| Notes: | | |

# Visitation Details

| Date: | M  T  W  T  F  S  S |
|---|---|
| Child(ren)'s name: | |
| Child(ren)'s age: | |

| Agreed Pick Up Time: | Agreed Drop Off Time: | |
|---|---|---|
| Actual Pick Up Time: | Actual Drop Off Time: | |
| Location: | Location: | |
| Custodian Name: | Relationship to child: | |
| Contact Info: | | Signature: |
| Witness Name: | | Signature: |
| Notes: | | |

| Date: | M  T  W  T  F  S  S |
|---|---|
| Child(ren)'s name: | |
| Child(ren)'s age: | |

| Agreed Pick Up Time: | Agreed Drop Off Time: | |
|---|---|---|
| Actual Pick Up Time: | Actual Drop Off Time: | |
| Location: | Location: | |
| Custodian Name: | Relationship to child: | |
| Contact Info: | | Signature: |
| Witness Name: | | Signature: |
| Notes: | | |

| Date: | M  T  W  T  F  S  S |
|---|---|
| Child(ren)'s name: | |
| Child(ren)'s age: | |

| Agreed Pick Up Time: | Agreed Drop Off Time: | |
|---|---|---|
| Actual Pick Up Time: | Actual Drop Off Time: | |
| Location: | Location: | |
| Custodian Name: | Relationship to child: | |
| Contact Info: | | Signature: |
| Witness Name: | | Signature: |
| Notes: | | |

# Visitation Details

| Date: | M T W T F S S |
|---|---|
| Child(ren)'s name: | |
| Child(ren)'s age: | |

| Agreed Pick Up Time: | Agreed Drop Off Time: | |
|---|---|---|
| Actual Pick Up Time: | Actual Drop Off Time: | |
| Location: | Location: | |
| Custodian Name: | Relationship to child: | |
| Contact Info: | | Signature: |
| Witness Name: | | Signature: |
| Notes: | | |

| Date: | M T W T F S S |
|---|---|
| Child(ren)'s name: | |
| Child(ren)'s age: | |

| Agreed Pick Up Time: | Agreed Drop Off Time: | |
|---|---|---|
| Actual Pick Up Time: | Actual Drop Off Time: | |
| Location: | Location: | |
| Custodian Name: | Relationship to child: | |
| Contact Info: | | Signature: |
| Witness Name: | | Signature: |
| Notes: | | |

| Date: | M T W T F S S |
|---|---|
| Child(ren)'s name: | |
| Child(ren)'s age: | |

| Agreed Pick Up Time: | Agreed Drop Off Time: | |
|---|---|---|
| Actual Pick Up Time: | Actual Drop Off Time: | |
| Location: | Location: | |
| Custodian Name: | Relationship to child: | |
| Contact Info: | | Signature: |
| Witness Name: | | Signature: |
| Notes: | | |

# Visitation Details

| Date: | | M | T | W | T | F | S | S |
|---|---|---|---|---|---|---|---|---|
| Child(ren)'s name: | | | | | | | | |
| Child(ren)'s age: | | | | | | | | |
| Agreed Pick Up Time: | Agreed Drop Off Time: | | | | | | | |
| Actual Pick Up Time: | Actual Drop Off Time: | | | | | | | |
| Location: | Location: | | | | | | | |
| Custodian Name: | Relationship to child: | | | | | | | |
| Contact Info: | | Signature: | | | | | | |
| Witness Name: | | Signature: | | | | | | |
| Notes: | | | | | | | | |

| Date: | | M | T | W | T | F | S | S |
|---|---|---|---|---|---|---|---|---|
| Child(ren)'s name: | | | | | | | | |
| Child(ren)'s age: | | | | | | | | |
| Agreed Pick Up Time: | Agreed Drop Off Time: | | | | | | | |
| Actual Pick Up Time: | Actual Drop Off Time: | | | | | | | |
| Location: | Location: | | | | | | | |
| Custodian Name: | Relationship to child: | | | | | | | |
| Contact Info: | | Signature: | | | | | | |
| Witness Name: | | Signature: | | | | | | |
| Notes: | | | | | | | | |

| Date: | | M | T | W | T | F | S | S |
|---|---|---|---|---|---|---|---|---|
| Child(ren)'s name: | | | | | | | | |
| Child(ren)'s age: | | | | | | | | |
| Agreed Pick Up Time: | Agreed Drop Off Time: | | | | | | | |
| Actual Pick Up Time: | Actual Drop Off Time: | | | | | | | |
| Location: | Location: | | | | | | | |
| Custodian Name: | Relationship to child: | | | | | | | |
| Contact Info: | | Signature: | | | | | | |
| Witness Name: | | Signature: | | | | | | |
| Notes: | | | | | | | | |

# Visitation Details

| Date: | | M   T   W   T   F   S   S |
|---|---|---|
| Child(ren)'s name: | | |
| Child(ren)'s age: | | |
| Agreed Pick Up Time: | Agreed Drop Off Time: | |
| Actual Pick Up Time: | Actual Drop Off Time: | |
| Location: | Location: | |
| Custodian Name: | Relationship to child: | |
| Contact Info: | | Signature: |
| Witness Name: | | Signature: |
| Notes: | | |

| Date: | | M   T   W   T   F   S   S |
|---|---|---|
| Child(ren)'s name: | | |
| Child(ren)'s age: | | |
| Agreed Pick Up Time: | Agreed Drop Off Time: | |
| Actual Pick Up Time: | Actual Drop Off Time: | |
| Location: | Location: | |
| Custodian Name: | Relationship to child: | |
| Contact Info: | | Signature: |
| Witness Name: | | Signature: |
| Notes: | | |

| Date: | | M   T   W   T   F   S   S |
|---|---|---|
| Child(ren)'s name: | | |
| Child(ren)'s age: | | |
| Agreed Pick Up Time: | Agreed Drop Off Time: | |
| Actual Pick Up Time: | Actual Drop Off Time: | |
| Location: | Location: | |
| Custodian Name: | Relationship to child: | |
| Contact Info: | | Signature: |
| Witness Name: | | Signature: |
| Notes: | | |

# Visitation Details

| Date: | | M T W T F S S |
|---|---|---|
| Child(ren)'s name: | | |
| Child(ren)'s age: | | |
| Agreed Pick Up Time: | Agreed Drop Off Time: | |
| Actual Pick Up Time: | Actual Drop Off Time: | |
| Location: | Location: | |
| Custodian Name: | Relationship to child: | |
| Contact Info: | | Signature: |
| Witness Name: | | Signature: |
| Notes: | | |

| Date: | | M T W T F S S |
|---|---|---|
| Child(ren)'s name: | | |
| Child(ren)'s age: | | |
| Agreed Pick Up Time: | Agreed Drop Off Time: | |
| Actual Pick Up Time: | Actual Drop Off Time: | |
| Location: | Location: | |
| Custodian Name: | Relationship to child: | |
| Contact Info: | | Signature: |
| Witness Name: | | Signature: |
| Notes: | | |

| Date: | | M T W T F S S |
|---|---|---|
| Child(ren)'s name: | | |
| Child(ren)'s age: | | |
| Agreed Pick Up Time: | Agreed Drop Off Time: | |
| Actual Pick Up Time: | Actual Drop Off Time: | |
| Location: | Location: | |
| Custodian Name: | Relationship to child: | |
| Contact Info: | | Signature: |
| Witness Name: | | Signature: |
| Notes: | | |

# Visitation Details

| Date: | M   T   W   T   F   S   S |
|---|---|
| Child(ren)'s name: | |
| Child(ren)'s age: | |
| Agreed Pick Up Time: | Agreed Drop Off Time: |
| Actual Pick Up Time: | Actual Drop Off Time: |
| Location: | Location: |
| Custodian Name: | Relationship to child: |
| Contact Info: | Signature: |
| Witness Name: | Signature: |
| Notes: | |

| Date: | M   T   W   T   F   S   S |
|---|---|
| Child(ren)'s name: | |
| Child(ren)'s age: | |
| Agreed Pick Up Time: | Agreed Drop Off Time: |
| Actual Pick Up Time: | Actual Drop Off Time: |
| Location: | Location: |
| Custodian Name: | Relationship to child: |
| Contact Info: | Signature: |
| Witness Name: | Signature: |
| Notes: | |

| Date: | M   T   W   T   F   S   S |
|---|---|
| Child(ren)'s name: | |
| Child(ren)'s age: | |
| Agreed Pick Up Time: | Agreed Drop Off Time: |
| Actual Pick Up Time: | Actual Drop Off Time: |
| Location: | Location: |
| Custodian Name: | Relationship to child: |
| Contact Info: | Signature: |
| Witness Name: | Signature: |
| Notes: | |

# Visitation Details

| Date: | | M  T  W  T  F  S  S |
|---|---|---|
| Child(ren)'s name: | | |
| Child(ren)'s age: | | |
| Agreed Pick Up Time: | | Agreed Drop Off Time: |
| Actual Pick Up Time: | | Actual Drop Off Time: |
| Location: | | Location: |
| Custodian Name: | | Relationship to child: |
| Contact Info: | | Signature: |
| Witness Name: | | Signature: |
| Notes: | | |

| Date: | | M  T  W  T  F  S  S |
|---|---|---|
| Child(ren)'s name: | | |
| Child(ren)'s age: | | |
| Agreed Pick Up Time: | | Agreed Drop Off Time: |
| Actual Pick Up Time: | | Actual Drop Off Time: |
| Location: | | Location: |
| Custodian Name: | | Relationship to child: |
| Contact Info: | | Signature: |
| Witness Name: | | Signature: |
| Notes: | | |

| Date: | | M  T  W  T  F  S  S |
|---|---|---|
| Child(ren)'s name: | | |
| Child(ren)'s age: | | |
| Agreed Pick Up Time: | | Agreed Drop Off Time: |
| Actual Pick Up Time: | | Actual Drop Off Time: |
| Location: | | Location: |
| Custodian Name: | | Relationship to child: |
| Contact Info: | | Signature: |
| Witness Name: | | Signature: |
| Notes: | | |

# Visitation Details

| Date: | | M | T | W | T | F | S | S |
|---|---|---|---|---|---|---|---|---|
| Child(ren)'s name: | | | | | | | | |
| Child(ren)'s age: | | | | | | | | |
| Agreed Pick Up Time: | Agreed Drop Off Time: | | | | | | | |
| Actual Pick Up Time: | Actual Drop Off Time: | | | | | | | |
| Location: | Location: | | | | | | | |
| Custodian Name: | Relationship to child: | | | | | | | |
| Contact Info: | | Signature: | | | | | | |
| Witness Name: | | Signature: | | | | | | |
| Notes: | | | | | | | | |

| Date: | | M | T | W | T | F | S | S |
|---|---|---|---|---|---|---|---|---|
| Child(ren)'s name: | | | | | | | | |
| Child(ren)'s age: | | | | | | | | |
| Agreed Pick Up Time: | Agreed Drop Off Time: | | | | | | | |
| Actual Pick Up Time: | Actual Drop Off Time: | | | | | | | |
| Location: | Location: | | | | | | | |
| Custodian Name: | Relationship to child: | | | | | | | |
| Contact Info: | | Signature: | | | | | | |
| Witness Name: | | Signature: | | | | | | |
| Notes: | | | | | | | | |

| Date: | | M | T | W | T | F | S | S |
|---|---|---|---|---|---|---|---|---|
| Child(ren)'s name: | | | | | | | | |
| Child(ren)'s age: | | | | | | | | |
| Agreed Pick Up Time: | Agreed Drop Off Time: | | | | | | | |
| Actual Pick Up Time: | Actual Drop Off Time: | | | | | | | |
| Location: | Location: | | | | | | | |
| Custodian Name: | Relationship to child: | | | | | | | |
| Contact Info: | | Signature: | | | | | | |
| Witness Name: | | Signature: | | | | | | |
| Notes: | | | | | | | | |

# Visitation Details

| Date: | | M T W T F S S |
|---|---|---|
| Child(ren)'s name: | | |
| Child(ren)'s age: | | |
| Agreed Pick Up Time: | Agreed Drop Off Time: | |
| Actual Pick Up Time: | Actual Drop Off Time: | |
| Location: | Location: | |
| Custodian Name: | Relationship to child: | |
| Contact Info: | Signature: | |
| Witness Name: | Signature: | |
| Notes: | | |

| Date: | | M T W T F S S |
|---|---|---|
| Child(ren)'s name: | | |
| Child(ren)'s age: | | |
| Agreed Pick Up Time: | Agreed Drop Off Time: | |
| Actual Pick Up Time: | Actual Drop Off Time: | |
| Location: | Location: | |
| Custodian Name: | Relationship to child: | |
| Contact Info: | Signature: | |
| Witness Name: | Signature: | |
| Notes: | | |

| Date: | | M T W T F S S |
|---|---|---|
| Child(ren)'s name: | | |
| Child(ren)'s age: | | |
| Agreed Pick Up Time: | Agreed Drop Off Time: | |
| Actual Pick Up Time: | Actual Drop Off Time: | |
| Location: | Location: | |
| Custodian Name: | Relationship to child: | |
| Contact Info: | Signature: | |
| Witness Name: | Signature: | |
| Notes: | | |

# Visitation Details

| Date: | | M   T   W   T   F   S   S |
|---|---|---|
| Child(ren)'s name: | | |
| Child(ren)'s age: | | |
| Agreed Pick Up Time: | | Agreed Drop Off Time: |
| Actual Pick Up Time: | | Actual Drop Off Time: |
| Location: | | Location: |
| Custodian Name: | | Relationship to child: |
| Contact Info: | | Signature: |
| Witness Name: | | Signature: |
| Notes: | | |

| Date: | | M   T   W   T   F   S   S |
|---|---|---|
| Child(ren)'s name: | | |
| Child(ren)'s age: | | |
| Agreed Pick Up Time: | | Agreed Drop Off Time: |
| Actual Pick Up Time: | | Actual Drop Off Time: |
| Location: | | Location: |
| Custodian Name: | | Relationship to child: |
| Contact Info: | | Signature: |
| Witness Name: | | Signature: |
| Notes: | | |

| Date: | | M   T   W   T   F   S   S |
|---|---|---|
| Child(ren)'s name: | | |
| Child(ren)'s age: | | |
| Agreed Pick Up Time: | | Agreed Drop Off Time: |
| Actual Pick Up Time: | | Actual Drop Off Time: |
| Location: | | Location: |
| Custodian Name: | | Relationship to child: |
| Contact Info: | | Signature: |
| Witness Name: | | Signature: |
| Notes: | | |

# Visitation Details

| Date: | | M  T  W  T  F  S  S |
|---|---|---|
| Child(ren)'s name: | | |
| Child(ren)'s age: | | |
| Agreed Pick Up Time: | Agreed Drop Off Time: | |
| Actual Pick Up Time: | Actual Drop Off Time: | |
| Location: | Location: | |
| Custodian Name: | Relationship to child: | |
| Contact Info: | Signature: | |
| Witness Name: | Signature: | |
| Notes: | | |

| Date: | | M  T  W  T  F  S  S |
|---|---|---|
| Child(ren)'s name: | | |
| Child(ren)'s age: | | |
| Agreed Pick Up Time: | Agreed Drop Off Time: | |
| Actual Pick Up Time: | Actual Drop Off Time: | |
| Location: | Location: | |
| Custodian Name: | Relationship to child: | |
| Contact Info: | Signature: | |
| Witness Name: | Signature: | |
| Notes: | | |

| Date: | | M  T  W  T  F  S  S |
|---|---|---|
| Child(ren)'s name: | | |
| Child(ren)'s age: | | |
| Agreed Pick Up Time: | Agreed Drop Off Time: | |
| Actual Pick Up Time: | Actual Drop Off Time: | |
| Location: | Location: | |
| Custodian Name: | Relationship to child: | |
| Contact Info: | Signature: | |
| Witness Name: | Signature: | |
| Notes: | | |

# Visitation Details

| Date: | | M    T    W    T    F    S    S |
|---|---|---|
| Child(ren)'s name: | | |
| Child(ren)'s age: | | |
| Agreed Pick Up Time: | Agreed Drop Off Time: | |
| Actual Pick Up Time: | Actual Drop Off Time: | |
| Location: | Location: | |
| Custodian Name: | Relationship to child: | |
| Contact Info: | Signature: | |
| Witness Name: | Signature: | |
| Notes: | | |

| Date: | | M    T    W    T    F    S    S |
|---|---|---|
| Child(ren)'s name: | | |
| Child(ren)'s age: | | |
| Agreed Pick Up Time: | Agreed Drop Off Time: | |
| Actual Pick Up Time: | Actual Drop Off Time: | |
| Location: | Location: | |
| Custodian Name: | Relationship to child: | |
| Contact Info: | Signature: | |
| Witness Name: | Signature: | |
| Notes: | | |

| Date: | | M    T    W    T    F    S    S |
|---|---|---|
| Child(ren)'s name: | | |
| Child(ren)'s age: | | |
| Agreed Pick Up Time: | Agreed Drop Off Time: | |
| Actual Pick Up Time: | Actual Drop Off Time: | |
| Location: | Location: | |
| Custodian Name: | Relationship to child: | |
| Contact Info: | Signature: | |
| Witness Name: | Signature: | |
| Notes: | | |

# Visitation Details

| Date: | | M  T  W  T  F  S  S |
|---|---|---|
| Child(ren)'s name: | | |
| Child(ren)'s age: | | |
| Agreed Pick Up Time: | Agreed Drop Off Time: | |
| Actual Pick Up Time: | Actual Drop Off Time: | |
| Location: | Location: | |
| Custodian Name: | Relationship to child: | |
| Contact Info: | Signature: | |
| Witness Name: | Signature: | |
| Notes: | | |

| Date: | | M  T  W  T  F  S  S |
|---|---|---|
| Child(ren)'s name: | | |
| Child(ren)'s age: | | |
| Agreed Pick Up Time: | Agreed Drop Off Time: | |
| Actual Pick Up Time: | Actual Drop Off Time: | |
| Location: | Location: | |
| Custodian Name: | Relationship to child: | |
| Contact Info: | Signature: | |
| Witness Name: | Signature: | |
| Notes: | | |

| Date: | | M  T  W  T  F  S  S |
|---|---|---|
| Child(ren)'s name: | | |
| Child(ren)'s age: | | |
| Agreed Pick Up Time: | Agreed Drop Off Time: | |
| Actual Pick Up Time: | Actual Drop Off Time: | |
| Location: | Location: | |
| Custodian Name: | Relationship to child: | |
| Contact Info: | Signature: | |
| Witness Name: | Signature: | |
| Notes: | | |

# Communication

| Date: | M T W T F S S |
|---|---|
| Time: | Type (Call/Text/Other): |
| Duration: | Reason: |
| Who initiated this conversation: | |

**Topic Discussed and Additional Info:**

..........................................................................................................
..........................................................................................................
..........................................................................................................
..........................................................................................................
..........................................................................................................
..........................................................................................................

| Date: | M T W T F S S |
|---|---|
| Time: | Type (Call/Text/Other): |
| Duration: | Reason: |
| Who initiated this conversation: | |

**Topic Discussed and Additional Info:**

..........................................................................................................
..........................................................................................................
..........................................................................................................
..........................................................................................................
..........................................................................................................
..........................................................................................................

| Date: | M T W T F S S |
|---|---|
| Time: | Type (Call/Text/Other): |
| Duration: | Reason: |
| Who initiated this conversation: | |

**Topic Discussed and Additional Info:**

..........................................................................................................
..........................................................................................................
..........................................................................................................
..........................................................................................................
..........................................................................................................
..........................................................................................................

# Communication

| Date: | | M  T  W  T  F  S  S |
|---|---|---|
| Time: | Type (Call/Text/Other): | |
| Duration: | Reason: | |
| Who initiated this conversation: | | |

Topic Discussed and Additional Info:

......................................................................................................................................

......................................................................................................................................

......................................................................................................................................

......................................................................................................................................

......................................................................................................................................

| Date: | | M  T  W  T  F  S  S |
|---|---|---|
| Time: | Type (Call/Text/Other): | |
| Duration: | Reason: | |
| Who initiated this conversation: | | |

Topic Discussed and Additional Info:

......................................................................................................................................

......................................................................................................................................

......................................................................................................................................

......................................................................................................................................

......................................................................................................................................

| Date: | | M  T  W  T  F  S  S |
|---|---|---|
| Time: | Type (Call/Text/Other): | |
| Duration: | Reason: | |
| Who initiated this conversation: | | |

Topic Discussed and Additional Info:

......................................................................................................................................

......................................................................................................................................

......................................................................................................................................

......................................................................................................................................

# Communication

| Date: | M  T  W  T  F  S  S |
|---|---|
| Time: | Type(Call/Text/Other): |
| Duration: | Reason: |
| Who initiated this conversation: | |
| Topic Discussed and Additional Info: | |

| Date: | M  T  W  T  F  S  S |
|---|---|
| Time: | Type(Call/Text/Other): |
| Duration: | Reason: |
| Who initiated this conversation: | |
| Topic Discussed and Additional Info: | |

| Date: | M  T  W  T  F  S  S |
|---|---|
| Time: | Type(Call/Text/Other): |
| Duration: | Reason: |
| Who initiated this conversation: | |
| Topic Discussed and Additional Info: | |

# Communication

| Date: | M  T  W  T  F  S  S |
|---|---|
| Time: | Type(Call/Text/Other): |
| Duration: | Reason: |
| Who initiated this conversation: | |

**Topic Discussed and Additional Info:**

...................................................................................................................................

...................................................................................................................................

...................................................................................................................................

...................................................................................................................................

...................................................................................................................................

| Date: | M  T  W  T  F  S  S |
|---|---|
| Time: | Type(Call/Text/Other): |
| Duration: | Reason: |
| Who initiated this conversation: | |

**Topic Discussed and Additional Info:**

...................................................................................................................................

...................................................................................................................................

...................................................................................................................................

...................................................................................................................................

...................................................................................................................................

| Date: | M  T  W  T  F  S  S |
|---|---|
| Time: | Type(Call/Text/Other): |
| Duration: | Reason: |
| Who initiated this conversation: | |

**Topic Discussed and Additional Info:**

...................................................................................................................................

...................................................................................................................................

...................................................................................................................................

...................................................................................................................................

...................................................................................................................................

# Communication

| Date: | M T W T F S S |
|---|---|
| Time: | Type(Call/Text/Other): |
| Duration: | Reason: |
| Who initiated this conversation: | |

**Topic Discussed and Additional Info:**

..................................................................................................................
..................................................................................................................
..................................................................................................................
..................................................................................................................
..................................................................................................................

| Date: | M T W T F S S |
|---|---|
| Time: | Type(Call/Text/Other): |
| Duration: | Reason: |
| Who initiated this conversation: | |

**Topic Discussed and Additional Info:**

..................................................................................................................
..................................................................................................................
..................................................................................................................
..................................................................................................................
..................................................................................................................

| Date: | M T W T F S S |
|---|---|
| Time: | Type(Call/Text/Other): |
| Duration: | Reason: |
| Who initiated this conversation: | |

**Topic Discussed and Additional Info:**

..................................................................................................................
..................................................................................................................
..................................................................................................................
..................................................................................................................
..................................................................................................................

# Communication

| Date: | M T W T F S S |
|---|---|
| Time: | Type (Call/Text/Other): |
| Duration: | Reason: |
| Who initiated this conversation: | |
| Topic Discussed and Additional Info: | |

| Date: | M T W T F S S |
|---|---|
| Time: | Type (Call/Text/Other): |
| Duration: | Reason: |
| Who initiated this conversation: | |
| Topic Discussed and Additional Info: | |

| Date: | M T W T F S S |
|---|---|
| Time: | Type (Call/Text/Other): |
| Duration: | Reason: |
| Who initiated this conversation: | |
| Topic Discussed and Additional Info: | |

# Communication

| Date: | M  T  W  T  F  S  S |
|---|---|
| Time: | Type(Call/Text/Other): |
| Duration: | Reason: |
| Who initiated this conversation: | |

**Topic Discussed and Additional Info:**

..........................................................................................................................................

..........................................................................................................................................

..........................................................................................................................................

..........................................................................................................................................

..........................................................................................................................................

| Date: | M  T  W  T  F  S  S |
|---|---|
| Time: | Type(Call/Text/Other): |
| Duration: | Reason: |
| Who initiated this conversation: | |

**Topic Discussed and Additional Info:**

..........................................................................................................................................

..........................................................................................................................................

..........................................................................................................................................

..........................................................................................................................................

..........................................................................................................................................

| Date: | M  T  W  T  F  S  S |
|---|---|
| Time: | Type(Call/Text/Other): |
| Duration: | Reason: |
| Who initiated this conversation: | |

**Topic Discussed and Additional Info:**

..........................................................................................................................................

..........................................................................................................................................

..........................................................................................................................................

..........................................................................................................................................

..........................................................................................................................................

# Communication

| Date: | M  T  W  T  F  S  S |
|---|---|
| Time: | Type (Call/Text/Other): |
| Duration: | Reason: |
| Who initiated this conversation: | |

**Topic Discussed and Additional Info:**

...............................................................................................................................................

...............................................................................................................................................

...............................................................................................................................................

...............................................................................................................................................

...............................................................................................................................................

| Date: | M  T  W  T  F  S  S |
|---|---|
| Time: | Type (Call/Text/Other): |
| Duration: | Reason: |
| Who initiated this conversation: | |

**Topic Discussed and Additional Info:**

...............................................................................................................................................

...............................................................................................................................................

...............................................................................................................................................

...............................................................................................................................................

...............................................................................................................................................

| Date: | M  T  W  T  F  S  S |
|---|---|
| Time: | Type (Call/Text/Other): |
| Duration: | Reason: |
| Who initiated this conversation: | |

**Topic Discussed and Additional Info:**

...............................................................................................................................................

...............................................................................................................................................

...............................................................................................................................................

...............................................................................................................................................

...............................................................................................................................................

# Communication

| Date: | M   T   W   T   F   S   S |
|---|---|
| Time: | Type (Call/Text/Other): |
| Duration: | Reason: |
| Who initiated this conversation: | |

**Topic Discussed and Additional Info:**

| Date: | M   T   W   T   F   S   S |
|---|---|
| Time: | Type (Call/Text/Other): |
| Duration: | Reason: |
| Who initiated this conversation: | |

**Topic Discussed and Additional Info:**

| Date: | M   T   W   T   F   S   S |
|---|---|
| Time: | Type (Call/Text/Other): |
| Duration: | Reason: |
| Who initiated this conversation: | |

**Topic Discussed and Additional Info:**

# Communication

| Date: | M T W T F S S |
|---|---|
| Time: | Type(Call/Text/Other): |
| Duration: | Reason: |
| Who initiated this conversation: | |

**Topic Discussed and Additional Info:**

....................................................................................................
....................................................................................................
....................................................................................................
....................................................................................................
....................................................................................................
....................................................................................................

| Date: | M T W T F S S |
|---|---|
| Time: | Type(Call/Text/Other): |
| Duration: | Reason: |
| Who initiated this conversation: | |

**Topic Discussed and Additional Info:**

....................................................................................................
....................................................................................................
....................................................................................................
....................................................................................................
....................................................................................................
....................................................................................................

| Date: | M T W T F S S |
|---|---|
| Time: | Type(Call/Text/Other): |
| Duration: | Reason: |
| Who initiated this conversation: | |

**Topic Discussed and Additional Info:**

....................................................................................................
....................................................................................................
....................................................................................................
....................................................................................................
....................................................................................................

# Communication

| Date: | M T W T F S S |
|---|---|
| Time: | Type(Call/Text/Other): |
| Duration: | Reason: |
| Who initiated this conversation: | |

**Topic Discussed and Additional Info:**
........................................................................................................................
........................................................................................................................
........................................................................................................................
........................................................................................................................
........................................................................................................................
........................................................................................................................

| Date: | M T W T F S S |
|---|---|
| Time: | Type(Call/Text/Other): |
| Duration: | Reason: |
| Who initiated this conversation: | |

**Topic Discussed and Additional Info:**
........................................................................................................................
........................................................................................................................
........................................................................................................................
........................................................................................................................
........................................................................................................................
........................................................................................................................

| Date: | M T W T F S S |
|---|---|
| Time: | Type(Call/Text/Other): |
| Duration: | Reason: |
| Who initiated this conversation: | |

**Topic Discussed and Additional Info:**
........................................................................................................................
........................................................................................................................
........................................................................................................................
........................................................................................................................
........................................................................................................................
........................................................................................................................

# Communication

| Date: | M   T   W   T   F   S   S |
|---|---|
| Time: | Type(Call/Text/Other): |
| Duration: | Reason: |
| Who initiated this conversation: | |

Topic Discussed and Additional Info:

....................................................................................................

....................................................................................................

....................................................................................................

....................................................................................................

....................................................................................................

....................................................................................................

| Date: | M   T   W   T   F   S   S |
|---|---|
| Time: | Type(Call/Text/Other): |
| Duration: | Reason: |
| Who initiated this conversation: | |

Topic Discussed and Additional Info:

....................................................................................................

....................................................................................................

....................................................................................................

....................................................................................................

....................................................................................................

....................................................................................................

| Date: | M   T   W   T   F   S   S |
|---|---|
| Time: | Type(Call/Text/Other): |
| Duration: | Reason: |
| Who initiated this conversation: | |

Topic Discussed and Additional Info:

....................................................................................................

....................................................................................................

....................................................................................................

....................................................................................................

....................................................................................................

# Communication

| Date: | M  T  W  T  F  S  S |
|---|---|
| Time: | Type(Call/Text/Other): |
| Duration: | Reason: |
| Who initiated this conversation: | |

**Topic Discussed and Additional Info:**

...........................................................................................................................................

...........................................................................................................................................

...........................................................................................................................................

...........................................................................................................................................

...........................................................................................................................................

| Date: | M  T  W  T  F  S  S |
|---|---|
| Time: | Type(Call/Text/Other): |
| Duration: | Reason: |
| Who initiated this conversation: | |

**Topic Discussed and Additional Info:**

...........................................................................................................................................

...........................................................................................................................................

...........................................................................................................................................

...........................................................................................................................................

...........................................................................................................................................

| Date: | M  T  W  T  F  S  S |
|---|---|
| Time: | Type(Call/Text/Other): |
| Duration: | Reason: |
| Who initiated this conversation: | |

**Topic Discussed and Additional Info:**

...........................................................................................................................................

...........................................................................................................................................

...........................................................................................................................................

...........................................................................................................................................

...........................................................................................................................................

# Communication

| Date: | | M | T | W | T | F | S | S |
|---|---|---|---|---|---|---|---|---|
| Time: | Type(Call/Text/Other): | | | | | | | |
| Duration: | Reason: | | | | | | | |
| Who initiated this conversation: | | | | | | | | |
| Topic Discussed and Additional Info: | | | | | | | | |

| Date: | | M | T | W | T | F | S | S |
|---|---|---|---|---|---|---|---|---|
| Time: | Type(Call/Text/Other): | | | | | | | |
| Duration: | Reason: | | | | | | | |
| Who initiated this conversation: | | | | | | | | |
| Topic Discussed and Additional Info: | | | | | | | | |

| Date: | | M | T | W | T | F | S | S |
|---|---|---|---|---|---|---|---|---|
| Time: | Type(Call/Text/Other): | | | | | | | |
| Duration: | Reason: | | | | | | | |
| Who initiated this conversation: | | | | | | | | |
| Topic Discussed and Additional Info: | | | | | | | | |

# Communication

| Date: | M T W T F S S |
|---|---|
| Time: | Type (Call/Text/Other): |
| Duration: | Reason: |
| Who initiated this conversation: | |

**Topic Discussed and Additional Info:**

........................................................................................................................................................
........................................................................................................................................................
........................................................................................................................................................
........................................................................................................................................................
........................................................................................................................................................

| Date: | M T W T F S S |
|---|---|
| Time: | Type (Call/Text/Other): |
| Duration: | Reason: |
| Who initiated this conversation: | |

**Topic Discussed and Additional Info:**

........................................................................................................................................................
........................................................................................................................................................
........................................................................................................................................................
........................................................................................................................................................
........................................................................................................................................................

| Date: | M T W T F S S |
|---|---|
| Time: | Type (Call/Text/Other): |
| Duration: | Reason: |
| Who initiated this conversation: | |

**Topic Discussed and Additional Info:**

........................................................................................................................................................
........................................................................................................................................................
........................................................................................................................................................
........................................................................................................................................................
........................................................................................................................................................

# Communication

| Date: | M　T　W　T　F　S　S |
|---|---|
| Time: | Type (Call/Text/Other): |
| Duration: | Reason: |
| Who initiated this conversation: | |

**Topic Discussed and Additional Info:**

...........................................................................................................................................

...........................................................................................................................................

...........................................................................................................................................

...........................................................................................................................................

...........................................................................................................................................

| Date: | M　T　W　T　F　S　S |
|---|---|
| Time: | Type (Call/Text/Other): |
| Duration: | Reason: |
| Who initiated this conversation: | |

**Topic Discussed and Additional Info:**

...........................................................................................................................................

...........................................................................................................................................

...........................................................................................................................................

...........................................................................................................................................

...........................................................................................................................................

| Date: | M　T　W　T　F　S　S |
|---|---|
| Time: | Type (Call/Text/Other): |
| Duration: | Reason: |
| Who initiated this conversation: | |

**Topic Discussed and Additional Info:**

...........................................................................................................................................

...........................................................................................................................................

...........................................................................................................................................

...........................................................................................................................................

# Communication

| Date: | M T W T F S S |
|---|---|
| Time: | Type(Call/Text/Other): |
| Duration: | Reason: |
| Who initiated this conversation: | |

Topic Discussed and Additional Info:

....................................................................................................

....................................................................................................

....................................................................................................

....................................................................................................

....................................................................................................

| Date: | M T W T F S S |
|---|---|
| Time: | Type(Call/Text/Other): |
| Duration: | Reason: |
| Who initiated this conversation: | |

Topic Discussed and Additional Info:

....................................................................................................

....................................................................................................

....................................................................................................

....................................................................................................

....................................................................................................

| Date: | M T W T F S S |
|---|---|
| Time: | Type(Call/Text/Other): |
| Duration: | Reason: |
| Who initiated this conversation: | |

Topic Discussed and Additional Info:

....................................................................................................

....................................................................................................

....................................................................................................

....................................................................................................

....................................................................................................

# Communication

| Date: | M T W T F S S |
|---|---|
| Time: | Type(Call/Text/Other): |
| Duration: | Reason: |
| Who initiated this conversation: | |

**Topic Discussed and Additional Info:**

..................................................................................................................................
..................................................................................................................................
..................................................................................................................................
..................................................................................................................................
..................................................................................................................................

| Date: | M T W T F S S |
|---|---|
| Time: | Type(Call/Text/Other): |
| Duration: | Reason: |
| Who initiated this conversation: | |

**Topic Discussed and Additional Info:**

..................................................................................................................................
..................................................................................................................................
..................................................................................................................................
..................................................................................................................................
..................................................................................................................................

| Date: | M T W T F S S |
|---|---|
| Time: | Type(Call/Text/Other): |
| Duration: | Reason: |
| Who initiated this conversation: | |

**Topic Discussed and Additional Info:**

..................................................................................................................................
..................................................................................................................................
..................................................................................................................................
..................................................................................................................................
..................................................................................................................................

# Communication

| Date: | M  T  W  T  F  S  S |
|---|---|
| Time: | Type(Call/Text/Other): |
| Duration: | Reason: |
| Who initiated this conversation: | |

**Topic Discussed and Additional Info:**

........................................................................................................................................

........................................................................................................................................

........................................................................................................................................

........................................................................................................................................

........................................................................................................................................

| Date: | M  T  W  T  F  S  S |
|---|---|
| Time: | Type(Call/Text/Other): |
| Duration: | Reason: |
| Who initiated this conversation: | |

**Topic Discussed and Additional Info:**

........................................................................................................................................

........................................................................................................................................

........................................................................................................................................

........................................................................................................................................

........................................................................................................................................

| Date: | M  T  W  T  F  S  S |
|---|---|
| Time: | Type(Call/Text/Other): |
| Duration: | Reason: |
| Who initiated this conversation: | |

**Topic Discussed and Additional Info:**

........................................................................................................................................

........................................................................................................................................

........................................................................................................................................

........................................................................................................................................

........................................................................................................................................

# Communication

| Date: | M T W T F S S |
|---|---|
| Time: | Type (Call/Text/Other): |
| Duration: | Reason: |
| Who initiated this conversation: | |
| Topic Discussed and Additional Info: | |

| Date: | M T W T F S S |
|---|---|
| Time: | Type (Call/Text/Other): |
| Duration: | Reason: |
| Who initiated this conversation: | |
| Topic Discussed and Additional Info: | |

| Date: | M T W T F S S |
|---|---|
| Time: | Type (Call/Text/Other): |
| Duration: | Reason: |
| Who initiated this conversation: | |
| Topic Discussed and Additional Info: | |

# Communication

| Date: | M T W T F S S |
|---|---|
| Time: | Type(Call/Text/Other): |
| Duration: | Reason: |
| Who initiated this conversation: | |

**Topic Discussed and Additional Info:** ....................................................................
..........................................................................................................................................
..........................................................................................................................................
..........................................................................................................................................
..........................................................................................................................................

| Date: | M T W T F S S |
|---|---|
| Time: | Type(Call/Text/Other): |
| Duration: | Reason: |
| Who initiated this conversation: | |

**Topic Discussed and Additional Info:** ....................................................................
..........................................................................................................................................
..........................................................................................................................................
..........................................................................................................................................
..........................................................................................................................................

| Date: | M T W T F S S |
|---|---|
| Time: | Type(Call/Text/Other): |
| Duration: | Reason: |
| Who initiated this conversation: | |

**Topic Discussed and Additional Info:** ....................................................................
..........................................................................................................................................
..........................................................................................................................................
..........................................................................................................................................
..........................................................................................................................................

# Communication

| Date: | M T W T F S S |
|---|---|
| Time: | Type (Call/Text/Other): |
| Duration: | Reason: |
| Who initiated this conversation: | |
| Topic Discussed and Additional Info: | |

| Date: | M T W T F S S |
|---|---|
| Time: | Type (Call/Text/Other): |
| Duration: | Reason: |
| Who initiated this conversation: | |
| Topic Discussed and Additional Info: | |

| Date: | M T W T F S S |
|---|---|
| Time: | Type (Call/Text/Other): |
| Duration: | Reason: |
| Who initiated this conversation: | |
| Topic Discussed and Additional Info: | |

# Communication

| Date: | M T W T F S S |
|---|---|
| Time: | Type(Call/Text/Other): |
| Duration: | Reason: |
| Who initiated this conversation: | |

**Topic Discussed and Additional Info:**
................................................................................
................................................................................
................................................................................
................................................................................
................................................................................
................................................................................

| Date: | M T W T F S S |
|---|---|
| Time: | Type(Call/Text/Other): |
| Duration: | Reason: |
| Who initiated this conversation: | |

**Topic Discussed and Additional Info:**
................................................................................
................................................................................
................................................................................
................................................................................
................................................................................
................................................................................

| Date: | M T W T F S S |
|---|---|
| Time: | Type(Call/Text/Other): |
| Duration: | Reason: |
| Who initiated this conversation: | |

**Topic Discussed and Additional Info:**
................................................................................
................................................................................
................................................................................
................................................................................
................................................................................
................................................................................

# Communication

| Date: | M  T  W  T  F  S  S |
|---|---|
| Time: | Type (Call/Text/Other): |
| Duration: | Reason: |
| Who initiated this conversation: | |

**Topic Discussed and Additional Info:**

........................................................................................................................

........................................................................................................................

........................................................................................................................

........................................................................................................................

........................................................................................................................

| Date: | M  T  W  T  F  S  S |
|---|---|
| Time: | Type (Call/Text/Other): |
| Duration: | Reason: |
| Who initiated this conversation: | |

**Topic Discussed and Additional Info:**

........................................................................................................................

........................................................................................................................

........................................................................................................................

........................................................................................................................

........................................................................................................................

| Date: | M  T  W  T  F  S  S |
|---|---|
| Time: | Type (Call/Text/Other): |
| Duration: | Reason: |
| Who initiated this conversation: | |

**Topic Discussed and Additional Info:**

........................................................................................................................

........................................................................................................................

........................................................................................................................

........................................................................................................................

........................................................................................................................

# Child Support Ledger/Expenses Log

| Date | Payments, Expenses & Details | Amount | Notes |
|------|------------------------------|--------|-------|
|      |                              |        |       |
|      |                              |        |       |
|      |                              |        |       |
|      |                              |        |       |
|      |                              |        |       |
|      |                              |        |       |
|      |                              |        |       |
|      |                              |        |       |
|      |                              |        |       |
|      |                              |        |       |
|      |                              |        |       |
|      |                              |        |       |
|      |                              |        |       |
|      |                              |        |       |
|      |                              |        |       |
|      |                              |        |       |
|      |                              |        |       |
|      |                              |        |       |
|      |                              |        |       |
|      |                              |        |       |
|      |                              |        |       |
|      |                              |        |       |
|      |                              |        |       |
|      |                              |        |       |
|      |                              |        |       |
|      |                              |        |       |
|      |                              |        |       |
|      |                              |        |       |
|      |                              |        |       |
|      |                              |        |       |
|      |                              |        |       |
|      |                              |        |       |
|      |                              |        |       |

# Child Support Ledger/Expenses Log

| Date | Payments, Expenses & Details | Amount | Notes |
|------|------------------------------|--------|-------|
|  |  |  |  |
|  |  |  |  |
|  |  |  |  |
|  |  |  |  |
|  |  |  |  |
|  |  |  |  |
|  |  |  |  |
|  |  |  |  |
|  |  |  |  |
|  |  |  |  |
|  |  |  |  |
|  |  |  |  |
|  |  |  |  |
|  |  |  |  |
|  |  |  |  |
|  |  |  |  |
|  |  |  |  |
|  |  |  |  |
|  |  |  |  |
|  |  |  |  |
|  |  |  |  |
|  |  |  |  |
|  |  |  |  |
|  |  |  |  |
|  |  |  |  |
|  |  |  |  |
|  |  |  |  |
|  |  |  |  |
|  |  |  |  |
|  |  |  |  |
|  |  |  |  |
|  |  |  |  |
|  |  |  |  |
|  |  |  |  |
|  |  |  |  |
|  |  |  |  |

# Child Support Ledger/Expenses Log

| Date | Payments, Expenses & Details | Amount | Notes |
|------|------------------------------|--------|-------|
|      |                              |        |       |
|      |                              |        |       |
|      |                              |        |       |
|      |                              |        |       |
|      |                              |        |       |
|      |                              |        |       |
|      |                              |        |       |
|      |                              |        |       |
|      |                              |        |       |
|      |                              |        |       |
|      |                              |        |       |
|      |                              |        |       |
|      |                              |        |       |
|      |                              |        |       |
|      |                              |        |       |
|      |                              |        |       |
|      |                              |        |       |
|      |                              |        |       |
|      |                              |        |       |
|      |                              |        |       |
|      |                              |        |       |
|      |                              |        |       |
|      |                              |        |       |
|      |                              |        |       |
|      |                              |        |       |
|      |                              |        |       |
|      |                              |        |       |
|      |                              |        |       |
|      |                              |        |       |
|      |                              |        |       |
|      |                              |        |       |
|      |                              |        |       |
|      |                              |        |       |
|      |                              |        |       |

# Child Support Ledger/Expenses Log

| Date | Payments, Expenses & Details | Amount | Notes |
|------|------------------------------|--------|-------|
|      |                              |        |       |
|      |                              |        |       |
|      |                              |        |       |
|      |                              |        |       |
|      |                              |        |       |
|      |                              |        |       |
|      |                              |        |       |
|      |                              |        |       |
|      |                              |        |       |
|      |                              |        |       |
|      |                              |        |       |
|      |                              |        |       |
|      |                              |        |       |
|      |                              |        |       |
|      |                              |        |       |
|      |                              |        |       |
|      |                              |        |       |
|      |                              |        |       |
|      |                              |        |       |
|      |                              |        |       |
|      |                              |        |       |
|      |                              |        |       |
|      |                              |        |       |
|      |                              |        |       |
|      |                              |        |       |
|      |                              |        |       |
|      |                              |        |       |
|      |                              |        |       |
|      |                              |        |       |
|      |                              |        |       |
|      |                              |        |       |
|      |                              |        |       |
|      |                              |        |       |
|      |                              |        |       |

# Child Support Ledger/Expenses Log

| Date | Payments, Expenses & Details | Amount | Notes |
|---|---|---|---|
| | | | |
| | | | |
| | | | |
| | | | |
| | | | |
| | | | |
| | | | |
| | | | |
| | | | |
| | | | |
| | | | |
| | | | |
| | | | |
| | | | |
| | | | |
| | | | |
| | | | |
| | | | |
| | | | |
| | | | |
| | | | |
| | | | |
| | | | |
| | | | |
| | | | |
| | | | |
| | | | |
| | | | |
| | | | |
| | | | |
| | | | |
| | | | |
| | | | |
| | | | |
| | | | |
| | | | |

# Child Support Ledger/Expenses Log

| Date | Payments, Expenses & Details | Amount | Notes |
|------|------------------------------|--------|-------|
|      |                              |        |       |
|      |                              |        |       |
|      |                              |        |       |
|      |                              |        |       |
|      |                              |        |       |
|      |                              |        |       |
|      |                              |        |       |
|      |                              |        |       |
|      |                              |        |       |
|      |                              |        |       |
|      |                              |        |       |
|      |                              |        |       |
|      |                              |        |       |
|      |                              |        |       |
|      |                              |        |       |
|      |                              |        |       |
|      |                              |        |       |
|      |                              |        |       |
|      |                              |        |       |
|      |                              |        |       |
|      |                              |        |       |
|      |                              |        |       |
|      |                              |        |       |
|      |                              |        |       |
|      |                              |        |       |
|      |                              |        |       |
|      |                              |        |       |
|      |                              |        |       |
|      |                              |        |       |
|      |                              |        |       |
|      |                              |        |       |
|      |                              |        |       |
|      |                              |        |       |
|      |                              |        |       |
|      |                              |        |       |
|      |                              |        |       |
|      |                              |        |       |

# Child Support Ledger/Expenses Log

| Date | Payments, Expenses & Details | Amount | Notes |
|------|------------------------------|--------|-------|
|      |                              |        |       |
|      |                              |        |       |
|      |                              |        |       |
|      |                              |        |       |
|      |                              |        |       |
|      |                              |        |       |
|      |                              |        |       |
|      |                              |        |       |
|      |                              |        |       |
|      |                              |        |       |
|      |                              |        |       |
|      |                              |        |       |
|      |                              |        |       |
|      |                              |        |       |
|      |                              |        |       |
|      |                              |        |       |
|      |                              |        |       |
|      |                              |        |       |
|      |                              |        |       |
|      |                              |        |       |
|      |                              |        |       |
|      |                              |        |       |
|      |                              |        |       |
|      |                              |        |       |
|      |                              |        |       |
|      |                              |        |       |
|      |                              |        |       |
|      |                              |        |       |
|      |                              |        |       |
|      |                              |        |       |
|      |                              |        |       |
|      |                              |        |       |
|      |                              |        |       |
|      |                              |        |       |

# Child Support Ledger/Expenses Log

| Date | Payments, Expenses & Details | Amount | Notes |
|------|------------------------------|--------|-------|
|      |                              |        |       |
|      |                              |        |       |
|      |                              |        |       |
|      |                              |        |       |
|      |                              |        |       |
|      |                              |        |       |
|      |                              |        |       |
|      |                              |        |       |
|      |                              |        |       |
|      |                              |        |       |
|      |                              |        |       |
|      |                              |        |       |
|      |                              |        |       |
|      |                              |        |       |
|      |                              |        |       |
|      |                              |        |       |
|      |                              |        |       |
|      |                              |        |       |
|      |                              |        |       |
|      |                              |        |       |
|      |                              |        |       |
|      |                              |        |       |
|      |                              |        |       |
|      |                              |        |       |
|      |                              |        |       |
|      |                              |        |       |
|      |                              |        |       |
|      |                              |        |       |
|      |                              |        |       |
|      |                              |        |       |
|      |                              |        |       |
|      |                              |        |       |
|      |                              |        |       |
|      |                              |        |       |

# Child Support Ledger/Expenses Log

| Date | Payments, Expenses & Details | Amount | Notes |
|------|------------------------------|--------|-------|
|      |                              |        |       |
|      |                              |        |       |
|      |                              |        |       |
|      |                              |        |       |
|      |                              |        |       |
|      |                              |        |       |
|      |                              |        |       |
|      |                              |        |       |
|      |                              |        |       |
|      |                              |        |       |
|      |                              |        |       |
|      |                              |        |       |
|      |                              |        |       |
|      |                              |        |       |
|      |                              |        |       |
|      |                              |        |       |
|      |                              |        |       |
|      |                              |        |       |
|      |                              |        |       |
|      |                              |        |       |
|      |                              |        |       |
|      |                              |        |       |
|      |                              |        |       |
|      |                              |        |       |
|      |                              |        |       |
|      |                              |        |       |
|      |                              |        |       |
|      |                              |        |       |
|      |                              |        |       |
|      |                              |        |       |
|      |                              |        |       |
|      |                              |        |       |
|      |                              |        |       |

# Child Support Ledger/Expenses Log

| Date | Payments, Expenses & Details | Amount | Notes |
|------|------------------------------|--------|-------|
|      |                              |        |       |
|      |                              |        |       |
|      |                              |        |       |
|      |                              |        |       |
|      |                              |        |       |
|      |                              |        |       |
|      |                              |        |       |
|      |                              |        |       |
|      |                              |        |       |
|      |                              |        |       |
|      |                              |        |       |
|      |                              |        |       |
|      |                              |        |       |
|      |                              |        |       |
|      |                              |        |       |
|      |                              |        |       |
|      |                              |        |       |
|      |                              |        |       |
|      |                              |        |       |
|      |                              |        |       |
|      |                              |        |       |
|      |                              |        |       |
|      |                              |        |       |
|      |                              |        |       |
|      |                              |        |       |
|      |                              |        |       |
|      |                              |        |       |
|      |                              |        |       |
|      |                              |        |       |
|      |                              |        |       |
|      |                              |        |       |
|      |                              |        |       |

# Child Support Ledger/Expenses Log

| Date | Payments, Expenses & Details | Amount | Notes |
|------|------------------------------|--------|-------|
|      |                              |        |       |
|      |                              |        |       |
|      |                              |        |       |
|      |                              |        |       |
|      |                              |        |       |
|      |                              |        |       |
|      |                              |        |       |
|      |                              |        |       |
|      |                              |        |       |
|      |                              |        |       |
|      |                              |        |       |
|      |                              |        |       |
|      |                              |        |       |
|      |                              |        |       |
|      |                              |        |       |
|      |                              |        |       |
|      |                              |        |       |
|      |                              |        |       |
|      |                              |        |       |
|      |                              |        |       |
|      |                              |        |       |
|      |                              |        |       |
|      |                              |        |       |
|      |                              |        |       |
|      |                              |        |       |
|      |                              |        |       |
|      |                              |        |       |
|      |                              |        |       |
|      |                              |        |       |
|      |                              |        |       |

# Child Support Ledger/Expenses Log

| Date | Payments, Expenses & Details | Amount | Notes |
|------|------------------------------|--------|-------|
|      |                              |        |       |
|      |                              |        |       |
|      |                              |        |       |
|      |                              |        |       |
|      |                              |        |       |
|      |                              |        |       |
|      |                              |        |       |
|      |                              |        |       |
|      |                              |        |       |
|      |                              |        |       |
|      |                              |        |       |
|      |                              |        |       |
|      |                              |        |       |
|      |                              |        |       |
|      |                              |        |       |
|      |                              |        |       |
|      |                              |        |       |
|      |                              |        |       |
|      |                              |        |       |
|      |                              |        |       |
|      |                              |        |       |
|      |                              |        |       |
|      |                              |        |       |
|      |                              |        |       |
|      |                              |        |       |
|      |                              |        |       |
|      |                              |        |       |
|      |                              |        |       |
|      |                              |        |       |
|      |                              |        |       |
|      |                              |        |       |
|      |                              |        |       |
|      |                              |        |       |
|      |                              |        |       |

# Child Support Ledger/Expenses Log

| Date | Payments, Expenses & Details | Amount | Notes |
|------|------------------------------|--------|-------|
|      |                              |        |       |
|      |                              |        |       |
|      |                              |        |       |
|      |                              |        |       |
|      |                              |        |       |
|      |                              |        |       |
|      |                              |        |       |
|      |                              |        |       |
|      |                              |        |       |
|      |                              |        |       |
|      |                              |        |       |
|      |                              |        |       |
|      |                              |        |       |
|      |                              |        |       |
|      |                              |        |       |
|      |                              |        |       |
|      |                              |        |       |
|      |                              |        |       |
|      |                              |        |       |
|      |                              |        |       |
|      |                              |        |       |
|      |                              |        |       |
|      |                              |        |       |
|      |                              |        |       |
|      |                              |        |       |
|      |                              |        |       |
|      |                              |        |       |
|      |                              |        |       |
|      |                              |        |       |
|      |                              |        |       |
|      |                              |        |       |
|      |                              |        |       |
|      |                              |        |       |
|      |                              |        |       |
|      |                              |        |       |
|      |                              |        |       |

# Child Support Ledger/Expenses Log

| Date | Payments, Expenses & Details | Amount | Notes |
|------|------------------------------|--------|-------|
|      |                              |        |       |
|      |                              |        |       |
|      |                              |        |       |
|      |                              |        |       |
|      |                              |        |       |
|      |                              |        |       |
|      |                              |        |       |
|      |                              |        |       |
|      |                              |        |       |
|      |                              |        |       |
|      |                              |        |       |
|      |                              |        |       |
|      |                              |        |       |
|      |                              |        |       |
|      |                              |        |       |
|      |                              |        |       |
|      |                              |        |       |
|      |                              |        |       |
|      |                              |        |       |
|      |                              |        |       |
|      |                              |        |       |
|      |                              |        |       |
|      |                              |        |       |
|      |                              |        |       |
|      |                              |        |       |
|      |                              |        |       |
|      |                              |        |       |
|      |                              |        |       |
|      |                              |        |       |
|      |                              |        |       |
|      |                              |        |       |
|      |                              |        |       |
|      |                              |        |       |
|      |                              |        |       |
|      |                              |        |       |
|      |                              |        |       |

# Child Support Ledger/Expenses Log

| Date | Payments, Expenses & Details | Amount | Notes |
|------|------------------------------|--------|-------|
|      |                              |        |       |
|      |                              |        |       |
|      |                              |        |       |
|      |                              |        |       |
|      |                              |        |       |
|      |                              |        |       |
|      |                              |        |       |
|      |                              |        |       |
|      |                              |        |       |
|      |                              |        |       |
|      |                              |        |       |
|      |                              |        |       |
|      |                              |        |       |
|      |                              |        |       |
|      |                              |        |       |
|      |                              |        |       |
|      |                              |        |       |
|      |                              |        |       |
|      |                              |        |       |
|      |                              |        |       |
|      |                              |        |       |
|      |                              |        |       |
|      |                              |        |       |
|      |                              |        |       |
|      |                              |        |       |
|      |                              |        |       |
|      |                              |        |       |
|      |                              |        |       |
|      |                              |        |       |
|      |                              |        |       |
|      |                              |        |       |

# Child Support Ledger/Expenses Log

| Date | Payments, Expenses & Details | Amount | Notes |
|------|------------------------------|--------|-------|
|      |                              |        |       |
|      |                              |        |       |
|      |                              |        |       |
|      |                              |        |       |
|      |                              |        |       |
|      |                              |        |       |
|      |                              |        |       |
|      |                              |        |       |
|      |                              |        |       |
|      |                              |        |       |
|      |                              |        |       |
|      |                              |        |       |
|      |                              |        |       |
|      |                              |        |       |
|      |                              |        |       |
|      |                              |        |       |
|      |                              |        |       |
|      |                              |        |       |
|      |                              |        |       |
|      |                              |        |       |
|      |                              |        |       |
|      |                              |        |       |
|      |                              |        |       |
|      |                              |        |       |
|      |                              |        |       |
|      |                              |        |       |
|      |                              |        |       |
|      |                              |        |       |
|      |                              |        |       |
|      |                              |        |       |
|      |                              |        |       |
|      |                              |        |       |
|      |                              |        |       |
|      |                              |        |       |
|      |                              |        |       |

# Child Support Ledger/Expenses Log

| Date | Payments, Expenses & Details | Amount | Notes |
|------|------------------------------|--------|-------|
|      |                              |        |       |
|      |                              |        |       |
|      |                              |        |       |
|      |                              |        |       |
|      |                              |        |       |
|      |                              |        |       |
|      |                              |        |       |
|      |                              |        |       |
|      |                              |        |       |
|      |                              |        |       |
|      |                              |        |       |
|      |                              |        |       |
|      |                              |        |       |
|      |                              |        |       |
|      |                              |        |       |
|      |                              |        |       |
|      |                              |        |       |
|      |                              |        |       |
|      |                              |        |       |
|      |                              |        |       |
|      |                              |        |       |
|      |                              |        |       |
|      |                              |        |       |
|      |                              |        |       |
|      |                              |        |       |
|      |                              |        |       |
|      |                              |        |       |
|      |                              |        |       |
|      |                              |        |       |
|      |                              |        |       |
|      |                              |        |       |
|      |                              |        |       |
|      |                              |        |       |
|      |                              |        |       |
|      |                              |        |       |
|      |                              |        |       |

# Child Support Ledger/Expenses Log

| Date | Payments, Expenses & Details | Amount | Notes |
|------|------------------------------|--------|-------|
|      |                              |        |       |
|      |                              |        |       |
|      |                              |        |       |
|      |                              |        |       |
|      |                              |        |       |
|      |                              |        |       |
|      |                              |        |       |
|      |                              |        |       |
|      |                              |        |       |
|      |                              |        |       |
|      |                              |        |       |
|      |                              |        |       |
|      |                              |        |       |
|      |                              |        |       |
|      |                              |        |       |
|      |                              |        |       |
|      |                              |        |       |
|      |                              |        |       |
|      |                              |        |       |
|      |                              |        |       |
|      |                              |        |       |
|      |                              |        |       |
|      |                              |        |       |
|      |                              |        |       |
|      |                              |        |       |
|      |                              |        |       |
|      |                              |        |       |
|      |                              |        |       |
|      |                              |        |       |
|      |                              |        |       |
|      |                              |        |       |
|      |                              |        |       |
|      |                              |        |       |
|      |                              |        |       |
|      |                              |        |       |
|      |                              |        |       |

# Child Support Ledger/Expenses Log

| Date | Payments, Expenses & Details | Amount | Notes |
|------|------------------------------|--------|-------|
|      |                              |        |       |
|      |                              |        |       |
|      |                              |        |       |
|      |                              |        |       |
|      |                              |        |       |
|      |                              |        |       |
|      |                              |        |       |
|      |                              |        |       |
|      |                              |        |       |
|      |                              |        |       |
|      |                              |        |       |
|      |                              |        |       |
|      |                              |        |       |
|      |                              |        |       |
|      |                              |        |       |
|      |                              |        |       |
|      |                              |        |       |
|      |                              |        |       |
|      |                              |        |       |
|      |                              |        |       |
|      |                              |        |       |
|      |                              |        |       |
|      |                              |        |       |
|      |                              |        |       |
|      |                              |        |       |
|      |                              |        |       |
|      |                              |        |       |
|      |                              |        |       |
|      |                              |        |       |
|      |                              |        |       |
|      |                              |        |       |
|      |                              |        |       |
|      |                              |        |       |
|      |                              |        |       |

# Child Support Ledger/Expenses Log

| Date | Payments, Expenses & Details | Amount | Notes |
|------|------------------------------|--------|-------|
|      |                              |        |       |
|      |                              |        |       |
|      |                              |        |       |
|      |                              |        |       |
|      |                              |        |       |
|      |                              |        |       |
|      |                              |        |       |
|      |                              |        |       |
|      |                              |        |       |
|      |                              |        |       |
|      |                              |        |       |
|      |                              |        |       |
|      |                              |        |       |
|      |                              |        |       |
|      |                              |        |       |
|      |                              |        |       |
|      |                              |        |       |
|      |                              |        |       |
|      |                              |        |       |
|      |                              |        |       |
|      |                              |        |       |
|      |                              |        |       |
|      |                              |        |       |
|      |                              |        |       |
|      |                              |        |       |
|      |                              |        |       |
|      |                              |        |       |
|      |                              |        |       |
|      |                              |        |       |
|      |                              |        |       |
|      |                              |        |       |
|      |                              |        |       |
|      |                              |        |       |

# Child Support Ledger/Expenses Log

| Date | Payments, Expenses & Details | Amount | Notes |
|------|------------------------------|--------|-------|
|      |                              |        |       |
|      |                              |        |       |
|      |                              |        |       |
|      |                              |        |       |
|      |                              |        |       |
|      |                              |        |       |
|      |                              |        |       |
|      |                              |        |       |
|      |                              |        |       |
|      |                              |        |       |
|      |                              |        |       |
|      |                              |        |       |
|      |                              |        |       |
|      |                              |        |       |
|      |                              |        |       |
|      |                              |        |       |
|      |                              |        |       |
|      |                              |        |       |
|      |                              |        |       |
|      |                              |        |       |
|      |                              |        |       |
|      |                              |        |       |
|      |                              |        |       |
|      |                              |        |       |
|      |                              |        |       |
|      |                              |        |       |
|      |                              |        |       |
|      |                              |        |       |
|      |                              |        |       |
|      |                              |        |       |
|      |                              |        |       |

# Child Support Ledger/Expenses Log

| Date | Payments, Expenses & Details | Amount | Notes |
|------|------------------------------|--------|-------|
|      |                              |        |       |
|      |                              |        |       |
|      |                              |        |       |
|      |                              |        |       |
|      |                              |        |       |
|      |                              |        |       |
|      |                              |        |       |
|      |                              |        |       |
|      |                              |        |       |
|      |                              |        |       |
|      |                              |        |       |
|      |                              |        |       |
|      |                              |        |       |
|      |                              |        |       |
|      |                              |        |       |
|      |                              |        |       |
|      |                              |        |       |
|      |                              |        |       |
|      |                              |        |       |
|      |                              |        |       |
|      |                              |        |       |
|      |                              |        |       |
|      |                              |        |       |
|      |                              |        |       |
|      |                              |        |       |
|      |                              |        |       |
|      |                              |        |       |
|      |                              |        |       |
|      |                              |        |       |
|      |                              |        |       |
|      |                              |        |       |
|      |                              |        |       |
|      |                              |        |       |

# Child Support Ledger/Expenses Log

| Date | Payments, Expenses & Details | Amount | Notes |
|------|------------------------------|--------|-------|
|      |                              |        |       |
|      |                              |        |       |
|      |                              |        |       |
|      |                              |        |       |
|      |                              |        |       |
|      |                              |        |       |
|      |                              |        |       |
|      |                              |        |       |
|      |                              |        |       |
|      |                              |        |       |
|      |                              |        |       |
|      |                              |        |       |
|      |                              |        |       |
|      |                              |        |       |
|      |                              |        |       |
|      |                              |        |       |
|      |                              |        |       |
|      |                              |        |       |
|      |                              |        |       |
|      |                              |        |       |
|      |                              |        |       |
|      |                              |        |       |
|      |                              |        |       |
|      |                              |        |       |
|      |                              |        |       |
|      |                              |        |       |
|      |                              |        |       |
|      |                              |        |       |
|      |                              |        |       |
|      |                              |        |       |
|      |                              |        |       |
|      |                              |        |       |

# Child Support Ledger/Expenses Log

| Date | Payments, Expenses & Details | Amount | Notes |
|------|------------------------------|--------|-------|
|      |                              |        |       |
|      |                              |        |       |
|      |                              |        |       |
|      |                              |        |       |
|      |                              |        |       |
|      |                              |        |       |
|      |                              |        |       |
|      |                              |        |       |
|      |                              |        |       |
|      |                              |        |       |
|      |                              |        |       |
|      |                              |        |       |
|      |                              |        |       |
|      |                              |        |       |
|      |                              |        |       |
|      |                              |        |       |
|      |                              |        |       |
|      |                              |        |       |
|      |                              |        |       |
|      |                              |        |       |
|      |                              |        |       |
|      |                              |        |       |
|      |                              |        |       |
|      |                              |        |       |
|      |                              |        |       |
|      |                              |        |       |
|      |                              |        |       |
|      |                              |        |       |
|      |                              |        |       |
|      |                              |        |       |
|      |                              |        |       |
|      |                              |        |       |
|      |                              |        |       |
|      |                              |        |       |

# Month:

| Mon | Tue | Wed | Thu |
|-----|-----|-----|-----|
| | | | |
| | | | |
| | | | |
| | | | |

# Year:

| Fri | Sat | Sun | NOTES |
|-----|-----|-----|-------|
| | | | |
| | | | |
| | | | |
| | | | |

# Month:

| Mon | Tue | Wed | Thu |
|-----|-----|-----|-----|
|     |     |     |     |
|     |     |     |     |
|     |     |     |     |
|     |     |     |     |

# Year:

| Fri | Sat | Sun | NOTES |
|-----|-----|-----|-------|
| | | | |
| | | | |
| | | | |
| | | | |

# Month:

| Mon | Tue | Wed | Thu |
|-----|-----|-----|-----|
|     |     |     |     |
|     |     |     |     |
|     |     |     |     |
|     |     |     |     |

# Year:

| Fri | Sat | Sun | NOTES |
|-----|-----|-----|-------|
|     |     |     |       |
|     |     |     |       |
|     |     |     |       |
|     |     |     |       |

# Month:

| Mon | Tue | Wed | Thu |
|-----|-----|-----|-----|
|     |     |     |     |
|     |     |     |     |
|     |     |     |     |
|     |     |     |     |

# Year:

| Fri | Sat | Sun | NOTES |
|-----|-----|-----|-------|
| | | | |
| | | | |
| | | | |
| | | | |

# Month:

| Mon | Tue | Wed | Thu |
|-----|-----|-----|-----|
|     |     |     |     |
|     |     |     |     |
|     |     |     |     |
|     |     |     |     |

# Year:

| Fri | Sat | Sun | NOTES |
|-----|-----|-----|-------|
| | | | |
| | | | |
| | | | |
| | | | |

# Month:

| Mon | Tue | Wed | Thu |
|-----|-----|-----|-----|
|     |     |     |     |
|     |     |     |     |
|     |     |     |     |
|     |     |     |     |

# Year:

| Fri | Sat | Sun | NOTES |
|---|---|---|---|
| | | | |
| | | | |
| | | | |
| | | | |

# Month:

| Mon | Tue | Wed | Thu |
|-----|-----|-----|-----|
|  |  |  |  |
|  |  |  |  |
|  |  |  |  |
|  |  |  |  |

# Year:

| Fri | Sat | Sun | NOTES |
|---|---|---|---|
| | | | |
| | | | |
| | | | |
| | | | |

# Month:

| Mon | Tue | Wed | Thu |
|-----|-----|-----|-----|
|     |     |     |     |
|     |     |     |     |
|     |     |     |     |
|     |     |     |     |

# Year:

| Fri | Sat | Sun | NOTES |
|-----|-----|-----|-------|
|     |     |     |       |
|     |     |     |       |
|     |     |     |       |
|     |     |     |       |

# Month:

| Mon | Tue | Wed | Thu |
|-----|-----|-----|-----|
| | | | |
| | | | |
| | | | |
| | | | |

# Year:

| Fri | Sat | Sun | NOTES |
|-----|-----|-----|-------|
| | | | |
| | | | |
| | | | |
| | | | |

# Month:

| Mon | Tue | Wed | Thu |
|-----|-----|-----|-----|
|  |  |  |  |
|  |  |  |  |
|  |  |  |  |
|  |  |  |  |

# Year:

| Fri | Sat | Sun | NOTES |
|-----|-----|-----|-------|
| | | | |
| | | | |
| | | | |
| | | | |

# Month:

........................................................................................................

| Mon | Tue | Wed | Thu |
|-----|-----|-----|-----|
| | | | |
| | | | |
| | | | |
| | | | |

# Year:

| Fri | Sat | Sun | NOTES |
|-----|-----|-----|-------|
| | | | |
| | | | |
| | | | |
| | | | |

# Month:

| Mon | Tue | Wed | Thu |
|-----|-----|-----|-----|
|     |     |     |     |
|     |     |     |     |
|     |     |     |     |
|     |     |     |     |

# Year:

| Fri | Sat | Sun | NOTES |
|-----|-----|-----|-------|
| | | | |
| | | | |
| | | | |
| | | | |

# Month:

| Mon | Tue | Wed | Thu |
|-----|-----|-----|-----|
|     |     |     |     |
|     |     |     |     |
|     |     |     |     |
|     |     |     |     |

# Year:

| Fri | Sat | Sun | NOTES |
|-----|-----|-----|-------|
| | | | |
| | | | |
| | | | |
| | | | |

# Month:

| Mon | Tue | Wed | Thu |
|-----|-----|-----|-----|
| | | | |
| | | | |
| | | | |
| | | | |

# Year:

| Fri | Sat | Sun | NOTES |
|-----|-----|-----|-------|
| | | | |
| | | | |
| | | | |
| | | | |

# Month:

| Mon | Tue | Wed | Thu |
|-----|-----|-----|-----|
|     |     |     |     |
|     |     |     |     |
|     |     |     |     |
|     |     |     |     |

# Year:

| Fri | Sat | Sun | NOTES |
|-----|-----|-----|-------|
| | | | |
| | | | |
| | | | |
| | | | |

# Month:

| Mon | Tue | Wed | Thu |
|-----|-----|-----|-----|
|     |     |     |     |
|     |     |     |     |
|     |     |     |     |
|     |     |     |     |

# Year:

| Fri | Sat | Sun | NOTES |
|-----|-----|-----|-------|
| | | | |
| | | | |
| | | | |
| | | | |

# Notes

# Notes

# Notes

# Notes

# Notes

# Notes

# Notes

# Notes

# Notes

# Notes

# Notes

# Notes

# Notes

# Notes

# Notes

# Notes

# Notes

# Notes

# Notes

# Notes

# Notes

# Notes

# Notes

# Notes

# Notes

# Notes

# Notes

# Notes

# Notes

# Notes

Made in the USA
Monee, IL
12 October 2021